Romantic DORSET

MARK BAUER

HALSGROVE

First published in Great Britain in 2008

British Library Cataloguing-in-Publication Data
A CIP record for this title is available from the British Library

ISBN 978 1 84114 709 3

HALSGROVE
Halsgrove House
Ryelands Industrial Estate
Bagley Road, Wellington,
Somerset TA21 9PZ
Tel: 01823 653777
Fax: 01823 216796
email: sales@halsgrove.com
website: www.halsgrove.com

Printed and bound by D'Auria Industrie Grafiche, Italy

For Julie and Harry

INTRODUCTION

I am not a Dorset local, having first moved here in 1989, only to be tempted away again by the opportunity to live and work abroad. I returned in the mid-nineties, and settled here, and the county has provided the inspiration for my photography since then. I can honestly say that the scenery of my adopted county is at least as beautiful as any I've seen elsewhere in the world.

Perhaps its greatest attraction is that it manages to pack an awful lot of variety into a small area — from the modern development in the east of the county to the wild landscape in the west, and of course, the dramatic and world-famous 'Jurassic' coast, stretching from Old Harry Rocks to east Devon. Once away from the development in the east, and with no motorway running through it, the county remains largely rural and unspoilt.

The east of Dorset is characterised by the urban conurbation of Bournemouth, Poole and Christchurch, but although development has been rapid, with a huge impact on the natural landscape — hundreds of acres of buildings having replaced heathland — there are still plenty of picturesque areas. Poole Harbour, one of the largest natural harbours in the world, is breathtaking, and contains Brownsea Island and several other uninhabited islands. The nature reserves of Hengistbury Head and Stanpit Marsh provide a welcome relief from the urban sprawl of the conurbation and just north of the main development are the attractive market town of Wimborne and the Kingston Lacy estate.

Further north, the landscape is made up of rolling hills and scattered villages. The River Stour, a favourite subject of mine, enters Dorset in the north and winds its way through some beautiful countryside on its way to the sea at Christchurch. There is plenty of historical and archaeological interest here, too, with the iron age hill forts of Hod Hill and Hambledon Hill being two of the best known sites.

West Dorset has a more remote and isolated feel. I still find it amazing that you can leave one of the main roads such as the A35, and within a few minutes find yourself in a location like Eggardon Hill, which has an atmosphere of wilderness, totally removed from the modern world. Even the resort towns such as Lyme Regis at times feel a little wild, with winter storms sending waves crashing over the Cobb, the town's artificial harbour.

For many people, Purbeck and south Dorset have the county's finest scenery; the coast, with its unique geological features, was designated a World Heritage site in 2001. In both Portland and Purbeck stone quarrying has been a major industry, and there are picturesque villages built from the local stone, as is the romantic ruin of Corfe Castle. The resort towns of Swanage and Weymouth have a delightfully old-fashioned feel.

My favourite times for landscape photography are the beginning and end of the day, when low sunlight helps to reveal the form and texture of the land, and many of the photographs in this book were taken at these times. Pre-dawn and dusk, too, often provide lighting conditions which are particularly atmospheric.

People always seem to be interested in the equipment I use, so here it is. Until about two years ago, I was using film exclusively, usually 6 x 7cm transparency film, but occasionally 35mm if I needed a little more flexibility. More recently, however, I've been working digitally, using a Canon 1ds mark II and a 5D. The pictures in this book are a fairly even mix of film and digital shots. As regards filtration, I very frequently use a neutral density graduated filter to even out the difference in brightness between the sky and the land and occasionally a polariser to reduce glare and boost colour saturation.

I hope that you enjoy the photographs in this book.

Mark Bauer,
2008

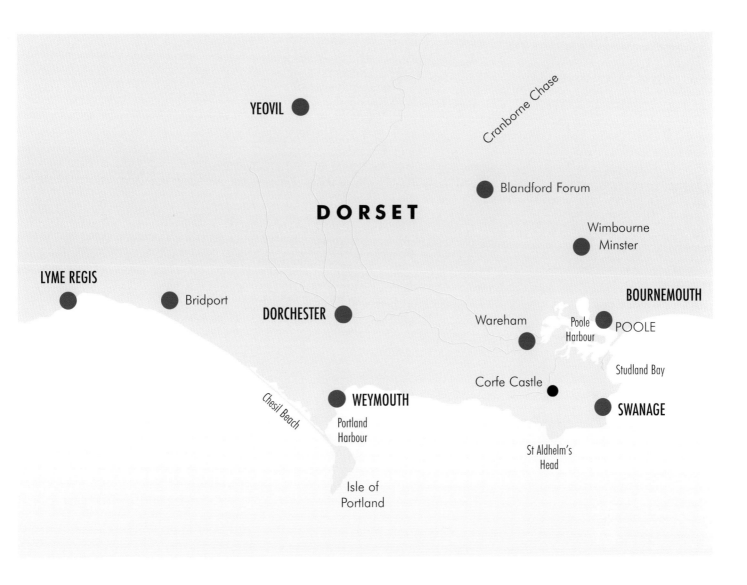

YEOVIL

Cranborne Chase

Blandford Forum

DORSET

Wimbourne
Minster

LYME REGIS

BOURNEMOUTH

Bridport

DORCHESTER

Wareham

Poole
Harbour

POOLE

Studland Bay

Corfe Castle

Chesil Beach

WEYMOUTH

SWANAGE

Portland
Harbour

St Aldhelm's
Head

Isle of
Portland

5

The sun rising over the Isle of Wight, from Avon Beach, Mudeford.

Swans are a common sight on the sea at Mudeford Quay.

Stanpit Marsh nature reserve, after a heavy frost.

Opposite:
Mudeford Quay is renowned among local photographers for its dramatic sunsets.

A glorious summer sunset over Christchurch Priory.

Opposite:
Sunrise at Stanpit Marsh, with Hengistbury Head in the distance.

As well as being a popular place for locals to escape from the urban sprawl of Bournemouth, Hengistbury Head is also an important archaeological site. Here, the late afternoon sunlight gives it a golden glow.

Opposite:
The first rays of sun on a winter's day light the boats on the river at Christchurch Quay.

Above left: A stormy sunset over Bournemouth, from Hengistbury Head.

Above right: Looking across Christchurch Harbour to Mudeford, from Hengistbury Head.

A clearing storm creates the conditions for a colourful sunset over Bournemouth Pier.

A winter sunset at Alum Chine, Bournemouth, with the Studland Peninsula in the background.

Opposite: A tranquil morning at Durley Chine, Bournemouth.

Looking towards Poole
from Branksome Chine.

The pastel colours of dawn at Branksome Chine.

Looking towards Old
Harry from Sandbanks.
A dramatic sunrise on
the longest day.

Opposite:
Sunset over Brownsea
Island, from Bramble
Bush Bay.

A light sea mist picks up the colours of the setting sun at Poole Harbour.

Opposite: Poole Harbour at sunset, with Brownsea Island in the background.

A completely still evening creates a mirror-like reflection of this boat in Poole Harbour.

A traditional red phone box stands rather incongruously among the sand dunes at Studland.

Late summer at
Studland Heath.

A summer sunset at Studland.

Daybreak at Shell Bay, Studland.

Pages 30-31:
Old Harry Rocks, from
Knoll Beach, Studland.
These chalk stacks were
once joined to the Needles
on the Isle of Wight, and
erosion is still very active.

A heavy evening sky over Bramble Bush Bay, near the chain ferry at Studland.

The twin towers of Wimborne Minster, viewed from across the Stour on a misty morning.

Opposite: A closer view of Old Harry Rocks.

Eyebridge, just up the
Stour from Wimborne.

Sunset over the
River Stour,
near Cowgrove.

Kingston Lacy House,
now owned by the
National Trust, was the
home of the Bankes family,
who had owned Corfe Castle
until it was destroyed
in the Civil War.

Opposite:
The gardens at
Kingston Lacy are well
known for snowdrops.

36

Pamphill is a beautiful,
unspoilt village on the
Kingston Lacy estate.

Opposite:
The bluebell wood at
Pamphill, on the
Kingston Lacy estate.

The beech avenue near Badbury Rings, north of Wimborne.

A poppy field near Knowlton, just south of Cranborne.

41

A frosty morning at Knowlton Church. The fourteenth century church was built inside a
Bronze Age earth circle. It was abandoned in the eighteenth century, when the roof collapsed.

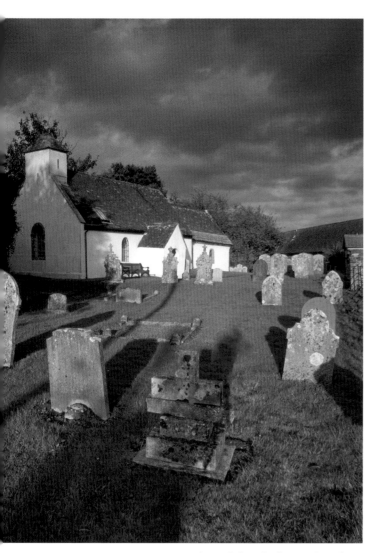

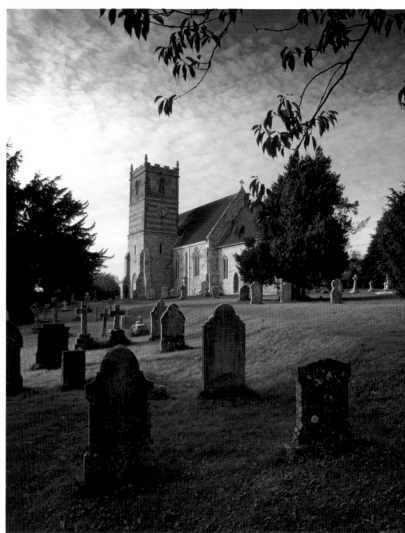

Above left: Chalbury Church is in a beautiful setting near Horton.

Above right: Gussage All Saints.

The winter sun, rising through mist over the Stour near Spetisbury.

Opposite:
A spectacular sunrise over the River Stour near Wimborne.

A misty morning near Cowgrove on the River Stour.

Opposite: Spetisbury, a village huddled on the banks of the River Stour.

Crawford Bridge at Spetisbury.

Sunrise over the flood plains of the Stour, after the river burst its banks following heavy rainfall.

Fishing is still an important part of daily life in Mudeford.

Looking north from the iron age hillfort of Hod Hill, on a misty autumn dawn.

The ramparts of Hod Hill.

Just down the road from Hod Hill is another hill fort, Hambledon Hill,
with the late afternoon sunshine revealing its shape in this shot.

A heavy frost on the banks of the Stour at Sturminster Newton Mill.

Opposite:
Sturminster Newton bridge
on a frosty morning.

The Tarrant is a tributary
of the River Stour, and there
is a series of attractive
villages alongside it…

…one of which is
Tarrant Monkton.

57

Ackling Dyke, one of the most spectacular Roman roads in Britain.

Right: Looking north across Cranborne Chase, from Gussage Hill.

A spectacular evening sky above one of the tumuli on the top of Gussage Hill.

Sunset over Cranborne Chase.

This shot was taken along the route of the Dorset Cursus, a 6-mile Neolithic enclosure. Why it was built is still a mystery, though the most popular theory is that it was a processional route.

Opposite:
Ashmore, in the north of the county, is the highest village in Dorset.

A peaceful scene in the Blackmore Vale, with the obelisk in Thornhill Park visible in the distance.

Opposite: A winter sunset over Melbury Hill.

A swan poses obligingly on the River Frome near Dorchester.

Opposite:
The derelict Cutt Mill at Hinton St Mary on a peaceful winter evening.

Maiden Castle, the iron age hill fort on the outskirts of Dorchester.

The brick garden at
Kingston Maurward House.
Kingston Maurward is now
a horticultural college.

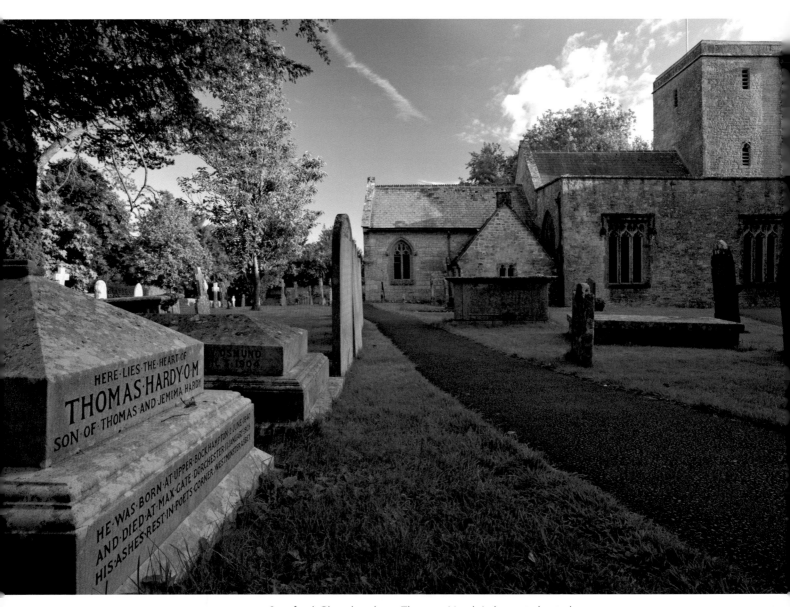

Stinsford Church, where Thomas Hardy's heart is buried.

The bridge at Lower Bockhampton, in the heart of Hardy country.

Storm clouds gather over Weymouth, viewed from Osmington Mills.

The stones on the beach at Osmington Mills, glowing in late afternoon sunshine.

Pages 74-75: Sunrise at Weymouth.

The lighthouse at Portland Bill, on the last day of summer.

A winter dusk at Portland Bill.

Came House and Church, Winterborne Came. The Dorset poet, William Barnes, was rector of the parish

Moonrise over the Fleet,
near Abbotsbury.

79

St Catherine's Chapel, Abbotsbury,
in late afternoon sunlight.

St Catherine's Chapel, from across the Fleet.

Sunset, Chesil Bank. Chesil Bank is an 8 mile ridge of shingle, which runs from Abbotsbury to Portland, forming a lagoon of partly salt, partly fresh water.

The Lookout, on top of
Puncknowle Knoll.

Sherborne Old Castle, which was owned by Sir Walter Raleigh. It is now managed by English Heritage.

The waterfall at Bride Head, the start of the Bride Valley.

Dappled sunlight on the hills enclosing the Bride Valley.

A stormy sky over the Bride Valley

Up Cerne on a sunny autumn afternoon.

The tiny hamlet of Nether Cerne,
with its mediaeval church.

Looking southeast from
Pilsdon Pen, the highest
point in Dorset, at dawn.

Looking south from Pilsdon Pen, with the conically-shaped Colmer's Hill in the distance.

The East Cliff at West Bay takes on a golden glow in the late afternoon sun.

Looking towards Lyme Regis from
Charmouth, at dusk.

Left:
Looking west from underneath
the cliffs at Burton Bradstock,
which have been carved by
the elements.

As rain clouds clear,
a rainbow appears
over Golden Cap.

The moon rising over the
hill fort of Eggardon Hill.
As well as having spectacular
views, it is an extremely
atmospheric location.

Opposite:
A clearing storm over Eggardon Hill.

The Cobb, Lyme Regis, at dawn. This harbour wall was famously used in the
opening scene of the film *The French Lieutenant's Woman*.

A summer sunrise over Lyme Regis Harbour.

The hills above Lyme Regis, rising above a summer mist.

Swanage Bay from Ballard Down, in late afternoon sunshine.

Brownsea Island is just
visible in the distance, in this
view from Ballard Down
on a misty morning.

A summer's evening at Handfast Point, Studland.

Opposite:
A fisherman watches the sunrise from the end of Swanage Pier.

The remains of Swanage Old Pier, rising through the mist on a winter's afternoon.

Dawn over Swanage.
To the left of the picture is
the Wellington Clock Tower,
which was moved to Swanage
from London in 1866, because
it was a traffic hazard.

Sunrise at Peveril Point.

Looking across Durlston Bay
towards the Castle, at sunset.

109

Rough seas at Winspit, a disused quarry
on the cliffs near Worth Matravers.

Left: Anvil Point lighthouse, in Durlston Country Park
in late afternoon light in winter.

Chapman's Pool is a delightful cove west of Swanage. Because access takes some effort, it is usually quiet. The distinctive shape of Houns-tout cliff is silhouetted against the dusk sky.

Opposite:
Looking west from Emmett's Hill, above Chapman's Pool.

Waves crashing onto the rocky ledges at Seacombe.

Opposite:
The duck pond at Worth Matravers, a picturesque village in Purbeck.

The cliffs at Dancing Ledge,
glowing in the winter sun.

An ammonite in the rocks at Dancing Ledge.

An autumn dawn at
St Aldhelm's Head.

Opposite:
The coastguard cottages
at St Aldhelm's Head,
which were built in 1834.

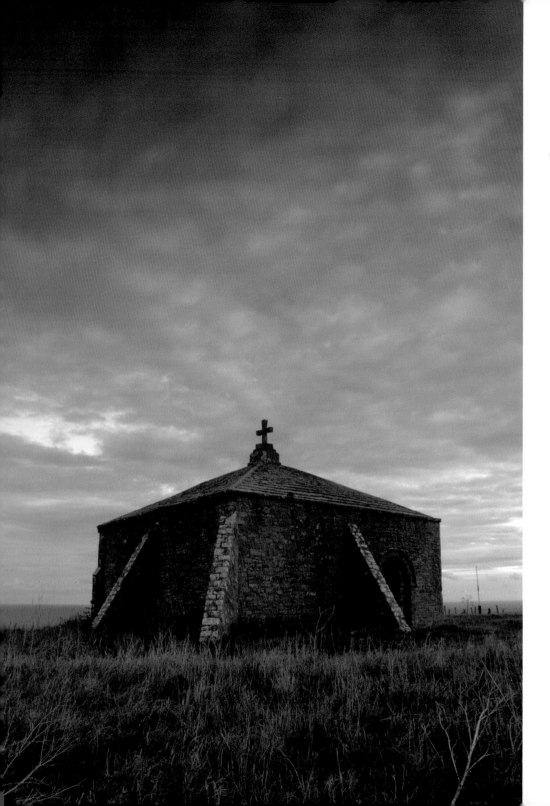

The isolated Norman chapel at St Aldhelm's Head, photographed under a brooding sky. The origins of the chapel are uncertain.

Opposite:
A gathering storm to the west of Chapman's Pool.

A spring dawn, with
the sun rising over
Corfe Castle.

Opposite:
An early morning mist
fills the valley below
West Hill, just outside
Corfe Castle.

Corfe Castle, viewed
from winter fields.

Opposite:
Looking across the Purbeck
Hills towards St Aldhelm's Head.

A light snowfall in
the Purbeck Hills.

Creech Grange, an impressive stone house built in the nineteenth century, lies at the bottom of the Purbeck Hills.

Woolbridge Manor, where Hardy's Tess supposedly spent her honeymoon. Note the inscription on the bridge.

Opposite:
The Blue Pool at Furzebrook, one of Dorset's hidden gems. The pool is a disused quarry, and the colour of the water is caused by mineral deposits.

The circular cove at Lulworth is a famous geological landmark, formed by coastal erosion.
It was photographed here just before the sun rose over its eastern flank.

Erosion has also formed this natural arch at Durdle Door, here lit by the last light of the setting sun.

Pages 132-133: Durdle Door: at certain times of year, the sun lights the rock as it sets, making it glow a golden colour.

Clavell's Tower, a folly built in the 1820s, is a well-known local landmark, and was the inspiration for the P.D. James novel, *The Black Tower.* It was perilously close to the cliff edge, and in danger of falling into the sea, but at the time of writing, is in the process of being moved some 25 metres back from the edge as part of a project organised by The Landmark Trust.

Opposite: This large rock off the coast near Durdle Door is known as 'The Bull'.

Clavell's Tower, viewed from
the western Ledges at Kimmeridge.

Opposite:
Looking west from the
Kimmeridge Ledges.

Worbarrow Bay, from the hill fort of Flower's Barrow. Worbarrow is near the deserted village of Tyneham, in an area used by the army as a firing range.

Worbarrow Tout, from the Bay. The Tout was used as a look-out by fishermen and coastguards, and there are fine views from there.

Looking west from Worbarrow Bay.

Opposite: Looking west from Flower's Barrow at sunset.

Above left: A spring morning on the River Frome, near the village of Tincleton.

Above right: A still morning, near Wareham.

Opposite: A frosty morning by the River Frome at Wareham.

Lady St Mary Church in Wareham, from across the Frome.